Da Rules:
The First One Hundred Plus Lessons I Learned In My Transition - Updated 2018

Shauna Marie O'Toole

ISBN: 978-1-387-67615-6

For my son, Sir Brendan Conor, knight errant,
Kingdom of Leinster, Eiri.

As you set forth, I offer you this thought.

Rule 39: *A ship in harbor is safe, but that's not
what ships are built for.* - John Shedd.

Fair winds and a following sea, my son.
May your own journeys be filled with wonders
and adventures!!

Forward:

Everyone needs a set of rules to live by - many of them are born out of experience.

Da Rules came about from things I learned while transitioning. This original idea came from an episode of *Star Trek: the next generation*. In this episode, a character had a running list of rules she had made as a result of experiences, both good and bad.

I thought that was a great idea!

Da Rules started to grow quickly once I started working on my memoir, *You Can't Shave In A Minimart Bathroom*.

Reading through the rules gives a peek into my world from Halloween 2003 to today, March 2018. How my world has changed! I started out as confused, but accepting that I was transgender. From there, it was a perpetual state of crisis caused by Puberty 2.0 and having to move 7 times in 22 months. Finally, to being an activist, public speaker, and becoming active in politics.

Da Rules:

Rule 1: Murphy's Law – Whatever can go wrong *will* go wrong.

Rule 2: O'Toole's Commentary – Murphy was an optimist.

Rule 3: By definition, all assumptions are wrong. But it may be all you have to go on.

Rule 4: The probability of something going wrong is directly proportional to the need for it to go right.

These first four rules govern the universe! Everything starts here. The rule I quote the most is actually Rule #3. This is the rule that everyone violates the most. It's the rule that causes the most angst, interpersonal difficulties, and generally causes the most amount of trouble for people.

Rule 8: Even if it can't go wrong, it still might.

Rule 9: When in doubt, trust your instincts.

Rule 10: Adapt or perish.

As I came out to my upper echelons, more and more people seemed to already know. As a result, bad research was done that potentially inhibited the end result. As a result, I had to adapt or perish.

Rule 11: It's never a bad time to ask *What Would Jesus Do*.

Or whatever deity you prefer. Asking *What Carl Sagan would do* is just as valid. Maybe even better since so many "Christians" use their belief system to persecute people like me - and, people are so surprised when I tell them that I do not subscribe to any formalized religion.

Rule 12: Transitioning is something you have to *feel* your way through. Thinking your way through life can leave you paralyzed.

Rule 13: When in doubt, talk with a professional

Rule 14: Dr. Jekyll cannot be separated from Ms. Hyde without killing both.

Transitioning is not an obviously logical process. It is highly emotional. Logical arguments can be made both to transition as well as to deny who you are. After all, I was an educated white male with every privilege that Society would allow. Transitioning would make me very much less than human in the eyes of Society - someone who is disposable. To many - *most!* - their logical solution would have been to deny who I was and to continue living a lie.

That is a 'logic' that makes everyone else happy, and leaves me a shell of a person.

No, the truly logical solution was to accept who I am. In accepting that I am a transgender woman, the cracks and wounds that had been open since early childhood started to heal. In accepting myself, I found a backbone that had been missing. In becoming whole, I now have a chance to make a difference in the world.

Rule 15: Dramatic, personal changes are more easily accepted by friends than by blood-family.

Rule 16: Your blood-family cannot be allowed to control your life. Trying to make everyone else happy will kill you in the process.

There are several family members who had great difficulty with my transition, but have since come around. Others have been banned and disowned because they took my former spouse's side in a very nasty divorce. As my father would have said, "Choices."

Rule 17: Stand strong.

Rule 18: Do your homework.

Rule 19: The more you use your intuition, the stronger it will become.

Rule 20: To win all, you have to bet all. Sometimes you have to risk the very things that are the most precious to you. It's a hard bet that tests your mettle to its core.

I have heard it said that there are always options. Sometimes, the best option is a gamble where you either win or lose everything. Sun Tzu in *The Art Of War* would describe this as being on Desperate Ground. It is both very liberating and very terrifying. Rule 20 and Rule 64 describe what it was like coming out to my children.

Rule 21: What you think about yourself is how it will be about yourself. If you think you are a victim, you will act like a victim. If you think you will succeed, you will succeed.

Rule 22: Be positive.

Rule 23: Don't go into any meeting without union representation.

There was an incident where I was called before the superintendent with legal and union muck-a-mucks. In that meeting, it became very clear that they were setting me up to fail. Within 48 hours, I had five legal organizations contacted and ready to come to my defense. When their verbiage changed, I concluded erroneously that they had become more supportive. (Rule 3 violation!) If they truly were supportive, why was I placed on a Teacher Improvement Program the very year I transitioned. Between not being protected by law and in the middle of Puberty 2.0, I eventually lost my teaching position.

Rule 24: Be flexible. Remember *Rule 7!* Whatever plan you create, it *has* to be adaptable or you are dead meat.

Rule 25: Every dark cloud has a silver lining. The converse is also true.

Rule 26: Be proud of yourself. Walk with your head held high.

Rule 27: It's better to be damned for who you are than loved for what you are not.

This goes hand in hand with Rule 14! So very many of us lose at least some of our family and friends because of our transition. It is very easy to feel very alone and isolated.

That feeling of isolation is one I know well. It is why I write and speak about my transition.

I want others to know that they are *not* alone on this journey.

Rule 28: Living and/or working at Condition One is exhausting. If you feel you have to be at battle stations all the time, you are existing – not living.

Rule 29: Let yourself cry.

Rule 30: Let yourself laugh.

Rule 31: Life is to be savored and enjoyed – not suffered through.

When I was growing up, the original *Star Trek* was first run. My friends and I all acted out whatever episode was shown that week. While it was fun to be Kirk or Scotty, the person I emulated in real life was Spock. Controlled. Unemotional. If I could control my emotions like a Vulcan, then I could keep this gender crisis I was feeling under control. One of the

9

difficult parts about my transition was learning how to feel again - how to express emotion again.

Rule 32: There is nothing to be ashamed of in being transgendered. Don't let others lay a guilt trip on you for being who you are.

Rule 33: The Almighty's job is to keep the panic out of your voice and give you a clear head so you can figure out what you need to do next.

Rule 34: *Everyone has a Ph.D. in MSU – Making Stuff Up.* Don Bennett, Eastman Kodak Company

Rule 35: *Happy are those who dream dreams, and are ready to pay the price to make them come true!* – Leon Joseph Cardinal Suenens.

Rule 36: Show me the data!

My counselor had figured out that I was transsexual long before I was ready to accept it. I am a scientist at heart. I need to see supporting information before I accept a radical idea.

I had the chance to live as my true self for a week. The inner resonance between body and soul was the data I needed to accept myself as being transsexual. It suddenly became when I transitioned, not if.

Rule 37: If you want to feel happiness and joy, you have to risk sadness and despair.

Rule 38: To find contentment, you must risk being at peace with yourself. To find wisdom, you must accept both halves of your psyche, and use them in equal measure.

Rule 39: *A ship in harbor is safe – but that is not what ships are built for.* **– John A. Shedd**

Rule 40: *When you pray for courage, God doesn't suddenly fill you up with courage. He gives you an opportunity to be courageous.* **– The Almighty.** *Evan Almighty.*

Deciding to be happy is a choice - a decision that requires courage. It does *not* mean that I am a Pollyanna believing that everything will work out okay because I believe that it will. That is new age clap-trap that is nonsense and that could get you killed. Present day Society does not like happy people. Why? Because happy people are harder to control!

Rule 41: *How do you change the world? One act of random kindness at a time.* **– The Almighty.** *Evan Almighty.*

How much better would our world be if we all simply acted with kindness towards one another?

Rule 42: *Dying is a day worth living for!* – **Captain Hector Barbossa.** *Pirate of the Caribbean – At World's End.*

Rule 43: *Today is a good day to die, but the day is not over.* **Lieutenant Worf,** *Star Trek: the next generation*

Rule 44: *It's not just about living forever, Jackie. The trick is living with yourself forever.* **Captain Teague to his son, Jack Sparrow.** *Pirate of the Caribbean – At World's End.*

Consider this question: If you had only 60 seconds left to live, how would you look back on your life? Would you think it was a life well spent - a life that made a difference? Or, would you look back wistfully at all the lost opportunities?

Back in my Before Days, I was a hand-wringing, indecisive wimp. I let others make decisions for me. This is what happens when body and soul are not in harmony.

Today, I have been told that I have a certain presence - that I tend to fill a room. I think this is a fair statement.

Rule 45: Perception is Reality!

Rule 46: If you want to hear the Almighty laugh, tell God your plans!

Rule 47: *Never "piss-off" the Easter Bunny.* – **Robert Curtis, Eastman Kodak Company**

I had the honor and privilege of working for Bob Curtis during my Kodak days. Together, we had the very best of adventures, and I was fortunate to realize that while I was working for him. This was one of his favorite phrases, and I have carried it on to this day.

Rule 48: *I think a man does what he can until his destiny is revealed to him.* – **Captain Algren.** *The Last Samurai*

Rule 49: *The sum of our answer is but this. We would not seek battle such as we are. Nor, such as we are, we will not shun it!* – **Henry V by William Shakespeare**

Rule 50: *When even one American -- who has done nothing wrong -- is forced by fear to shut his mind and close his mouth, then all Americans are in peril* – **Harry S Truman**

Rule 51: *The most powerful weapon on earth is the human soul on fire.* – **Ferdinand Foch**

Rule 52: *Nothing is stronger than the heart of a volunteer.* – **Lt. Colonel James Doolittle**

You will probably note a difference in tenor as you read through the rest of the rules. At this point in discovering my rules, I had become an activist - my heart still ablaze with the possibilities. Reality of the struggle ahead had not yet set in.

Today, years later, the reality of the struggle is there. I would like to believe that my heart is *still* ablaze with the possibilities!

Rule 53: *Don't let someone rent space in your head.* **Sarah Cliff**

Sarah and her husband Gareth are custodians where I used to teach. There were nights I was at school until almost midnight. They would stop by and talk as they cleaned the rooms. Solid good people. Back when I had but a few friends, they were solidly in my corner.

Rule 54: *The people who are trying to make this world worse are not taking a day off. How can I? Light up the darkness.* – **attributed to Bob Marley by Robert Neville,** *I Am Legend*

Rule 55: *How much of human life is lost in waiting?* – **Professor Harold Oxley.** *Indiana Jones and the Crystal Skulls.*

Rule 56: *Given the desire to do it, humans can accomplish almost anything.* – **Captain James Lovell, Commander Apollo 13**

This pretty well sums up why I do what I do!

Rule 57: *Just ignore everything they say and only pay attention to what they do.* **Professor Randy Pausch, Carnegie Mellon University**

Rule 58: *Brick walls let us show our dedication. They are there to separate us from people who really don't want to achieve their childhood dreams.* **Professor Randy Pausch, Carnegie Mellon University**

Rule 59: *Experience is what you get when you don't get what you want.* **Professor Randy Pausch, Carnegie Mellon University**

Rule 60: *It is better to fail spectacularly than to do something that is mediocre.* **Professor Randy Pausch, Carnegie Mellon University**

Rule 61: *Failure is not just acceptable, it's often essential.* **Professor Randy Pausch, Carnegie Mellon University**

Give yourself a gift. Take 90 minutes and watch *The Last Lecture*. Make sure it is the full presentation and not just an edited down version. Professor Randy Pausch had been diagnosed with pancreatic cancer. No cure. No stopping it. Doctors gave him 6 months to live. You would never have known it.

Carnegie Mellon University has a series where they ask professors what they would say if they had just one last lecture to give. Someone decided to record Randy Pausch as he gave what literally was his last lecture.

This is 90 minutes that can change your life for the better.

Professor Randy Pausch passed away almost a year later.

Rule 62: *I don't believe in the no-win scenario.* **Captain James T. Kirk.** *Star Trek: The Wrath of Kahn*

Rule 63: *Time is a companion that goes with us on the journey. It reminds us to cherish every moment, because they will never come again. What we leave behind is not as important as how we lived.* **Captain Jean**

Luc Picard. *Star Trek – Generations*

Rule 64: *Sometimes you have to roll the hard six.* **Admiral William Adama.** *Battlestar Galactica*

Rule 65: *The future doesn't belong to the faint hearted. It belongs to the brave.* **President Ronald Reagan addressing the nation after the loss of OV-99, the space shuttle** *Challenger.*

Since I transitioned, I believe I have been more alive than in the five decades previous. It takes courage to live an authentic life. Some of the most courageous people I have met are transpeople who have risked everything to live their true life. I hope I can live up to their example.

Rule 66: *Maybe the destination isn't what's important. Maybe it's the journey.* **Lieutenant Harry Kim,** *Star Trek Voyager*

Rule 67: *Living is not enough. You need something to live for.* **Admiral William Adama,** *Battlestar Galactica*

Rule 68: *I am not bound to win, but I am bound to be true. I am not bound to succeed, but I am bound to live by the light that I have. I must stand with anybody that stands right, and stand with him while he is right, and part with him when he goes wrong. –* **President Abraham Lincoln.**

Rule 69: *And in the end it's not the years in your life that count. It's the life in your years. –* **President Abraham Lincoln**

Rule 70: *Always bear in mind that your own resolution to succeed is more important than any one thing. –* **President Abraham Lincoln**

I don't know if it is age or reality setting in. What I do know is that this struggle for freedom is not going to end with the passage of the Gender Expression Non Discrimination Act. There are forces afoot trying to slowly rob all of us of our freedoms. Just look at the Patriot Act if you want an example.

Rule 71: *(Why do you want to be declared human?) To be acknowledged for who and what I am. No more. No less. Not for acclaim, not for approval. The simple truth of that recognition – this has been the elemental drive of my existence. And it must be achieved if I am to live or die with dignity.* **Andrew Martin**, *Bicentennial Man.*

When I first started coming out to friends and family, I gave them a copy of the late Robin Williams movie *Bicentennial Man*. The story is a fantastic metaphor for transitioning. This scene near the end of the movie always makes me cry. This is so much our struggle in the Trans

Community!

Rule 72: The process of accepting yourself is like being in a burning building. One group rushes out and gets on with their lives – and this is a very good thing. The second group is lost and confused – not knowing where to turn for help and rescue. The third group rushes back into the burning building to save as many as we can. We can't save everyone, but we can try. This third group is the one I want to belong to.

Rule 73: *We're all stories in the end. Just make it a good one, eh?* The 11th Doctor - *Doctor Who*

Rule 74: *I am* not *leaving my wingman!* – Pete "Maverick" Mitchell, *Top Gun*

Rule 75: *You go, we go!* – Lt. Steven McCaffrey, *Backdraft.*

Rule 76: *All that is necessary for the triumph of evil is for good men to do nothing –* **Edmund Burke**

Rule 77: *Your representative owes you, not his industry only, but his judgment; and he betrays both if instead of serving you he sacrifices it to your opinion. –* **Edmund Burke**

Rule 78: *It's a fine line standing behind a principal and hiding behind one. –* **President Whitmore,** *Independence Day*

Rules 76, 77, and 78 explain why I am running for office. I cannot stand aside and let someone else 'do something.' There is no guarantee that someone will! If not me, then who?

Rule 79: *The way I see it, life is a pile of good things and bad things. The good things don't always soften the bad things. But,* *vice versa, the bad things don't necessarily spoil the good things - or make them unimportant.* - **The 11th Doctor** - *Doctor Who*

Rule 80: *We can't be consumed by our petty differences anymore. We will be united in our common interests. Perhaps it's fate that today is the Fourth of July, and you will once again be fighting for our freedom... Not from tyranny, oppression, or persecution... but from annihilation. We're fighting for our right to live. To exist. And should we win the day, the Fourth of July will no longer be known as an American holiday, but as the day when the world declared in one voice: We will not go quietly into the night! We will not vanish without a fight! We're going to live on! We're going to survive! Today we celebrate our Independence Day!* – **President Whitmore**, *Independence Day*

Gay. Straight. Cisgender. Transgender. Republican. Democrat. Independent. We need to work together. There are far too many problems that we need to deal with immediately. Hiding behind political ideologies will not help us solve hunger, education, climate change and other issues.

Rule 81: *Assume good will.* **- Jeanne Gainsburg, The Out Alliance**

Rule 82: *There are three things you never talk about in polite company: sex, politics, and religion. Three things you often end up talking about if you are LGBT are sex, politics, and religion.* **- Scott Fearing, Former Director of the Out Alliance**

Most people are good, honest folk! Its when people get into groups of more than two that people start to act like pack animals.

Rule 83: Sometimes you have to throw away your most ardent cautionary rule and say, "Oh, what the hell. Let's do it!"

Rule 84: Never turn down an Adventure!

Rule 85: Adventures are always better when shared.

Rule 86: In a lifetime of adventures, it is the rare soul who realizes that they are having the *Adventure of a Lifetime*.

Suddenly you are a senior citizen. Retired. Do you seriously want to look back over your shoulder and wish you had made a different choices? Just try to stay out of jail while having your adventure!

Rule 87: It is better to have one or two close Friends with whom you trust your very life than a whole covey of acquaintances.

Rule 88: It is the fortunate parent who can also be friends with their adult children.

A few days ago, my son told me that he feels like we are friends as well as having the parent-child relationship. I was friends with my dad, and I am glad that I can keep this family tradition going.

Rule 89: Sometimes, you have to draw a line in the sand. Sometimes, you have to be on that line. Sometimes, you are a line of one.

Rule 89 has become my unofficial motto. Not only for my campaign, but for the outreach I do through my organization – The *We Exist Coalition of the Finger Lakes*.

My partner and I were watching the DVD of my favorite musical - *1776*. We were listening to John Adams played by incredible

William Daniels when a realization came to me.

"I sound and act a lot like John Adams."

She slowly and sadly nodded her head.

"Well, I guess there are worse role models to have," I replied.

Rule 90: Pay it forward.

Rule 91: Sometimes, it is the stranger you meet on your travels who will brighten your day. Sometimes, if you are fortunate, you get to be that stranger.

Rule 92: *If your dreams don't scare you, they are not big enough.* - Ellen Johnson Sirleaf

Rule 93: *Risk! Risk is our business!* - Captain James T. Kirk

Dream big! Dream bold! Living means taking a risk! Risk *is* our business! A life without reaching for the stars is simply existence.

There is an old joke about people in line to get through the Pearly Gates. Most were dirty and their clothing was tattered and torn, though there were a few who were dressed in their Sunday best.

St. Peter looked at those who were scruffy, checked his books, then joyfully welcomed them in to the Here After.

Those in their Sunday best stepped up to the gate. St. Pete check his lists then said that they couldn't come in.

"Why not?" one woman demanded to know.

"I went through all my books, and every one of you lived a quiet and safe life. You never lived. Kindly wait off to the side and we'll get to you when we have a chance."

That is my idea of purgatory.

Rule 94: *If you can't do something smart, then do something right.* **- Shepherd Derrial Book,** *Serenity*

Rule 95: So no *more running. I aim to misbehave!* **- Captain Malcolm Reynolds,** *Serenity*

There are those who say that we are an affront to society - that we need to conform. Pope Francis says that the Trans* Community is as much a threat to society as nuclear weapons!

To paraphrase Captain Reynolds, the Transgender Community is so done hiding. We are done running.

We aim to misbehave!

Rule 96: Live your life so that the Westboro Baptist Church will want to picket your funeral!

Rule 97: *Never cruel nor cowardly. Never give up. Never give in.* **- The Doctor,** *Day of the Doctor.*

Rule 98: *You can get better, or you can get bitter.* **- Reverend Dr. Karen Boyer.**

Rule 99: *When a transwoman is called a man, that is an act of violence.* **- Laverne Cox**

This is a simple denial of our identity. This is a declaration that we are no more than the mud that the ladder of success is placed upon. It is bigotry.

I've got news for you. We're not staying in the mud any longer!

Rule 100: *Then out spake brave Horatius, the Captain of the Gate: To every man upon this Earth; death comes soon or late. And how can a man die better than facing fearful odds; for the ashes of his fathers, and the temples of his gods.* **- Thomas Babbington Macaulay, The Lays of Ancient Rome**

Many years ago, I took Latin in high school with the late Nick Borrelli. I couldn't translate to save my soul, but I loved the stories! I think that was my only saving grace in that class.

Julius Caesar mentioned Horatius in one of his letters. The courage displayed has stayed with me. Seventy-two percent of all LGBTQ homicides are transwomen. Lets be honest and say that I get read as Trans* in about 1.74 seconds, +/- 0.03. I know that being out as a public speaker and politician places me at a greater risk. Hopefully, I am simply worrying about something that never happens. However, I listen to the rhetoric used against us. If the worse should happen and it advances our cause, then I am okay with it. If I can take an 'honor guard' with me, even better!

Rule 101: *Shame on the age and on its principles! The senate is aware of these things; the consul sees them; and yet this man lives. Lives! aye, he comes even into the senate. He takes a part in the public deliberations; he is watching and marking down and checking off for slaughter every individual among us. And we, gallant men that we are, think that we are doing our duty to the republic if we keep out of the way of his frenzied attacks.* **- Marcus Tullius Cicero, The First Catiline Oration**

Mr. Borrelli's class made a powerful impression on me! Catiline was plotting an overthrow of the Roman Republic. Cicero stood before the Senate and outlined each detail of the plot. Then, he lambasted the Roman Senate for turning their heads away from what they all knew was going on.

I listen to people use their religious beliefs as a way to justify their bigotry and hatred of those who are different. Not all, to be sure. However, enough do as to taint their faith systems. How often do we ignore bigotry because they say it interferes with their belief system? Freedom of Religion does not mean the rest of us have to bow to your beliefs. It means that others have to respect my belief system as well! You do not have the right to impose your faith system on me. You do not have the right to deny me services because we don't believe in the same things. I do not have the right to impose my faith system on you. There needs to be mutual respect to live our lives as we see fit.

Rule 102: *But if you look to our left, you will see that there is no one there. It's because we're the end of the line. The Union army stops here. We are the flank. Do you understand, gentlemen? We cannot retreat. We cannot withdraw. We are going to have to be stubborn today... The Reb army is going to swing around. It's gonna come up through that notch right over there. It'll move under the cover of trees, try to get 'round the flank. And gentlemen... we are the flank.* **- Colonel Joshua Lawrence Chamberlain –** *Gettysburg*

This struggle to regain our stolen rights and liberties is not just about the Transgender Community. This is a struggle for everyone's right to freely express themselves. What does it matter if I wear a skirt instead of slacks? How does that affect my ability to do my job? If its not a safety issue, it doesn't. It makes you nervous because I am being authentic? Perhaps there are unresolved issues that you need to address. What about people who are differently abled – both physically and mentally? Don't they have the right to marry without losing their benefits and support system. What about polyamorous families? Don't they have rights as well? For as long as there has been humans, there are those who have tried to maintain the status quo, and have oppressed those who stood up to them. Who, you might ask? Let me give you some examples. Gandhi. Jesus. Dr. King. Moses. If this is what it means to hold the flank against those who would oppress, then I am in the very best of company!

Rule 103: The Transgender Community is a leadership factory. - Rocky Acevedo

My beloved (now former) spouse hit the nail on the head. Being transgender is a tough gig. Survival requires that we advocate for ourselves. We have to stand up to those who would oppress us. We have to fight to keep our jobs. Facing odds like this can only bring out every leadership quality within a person. If there was any one phrase that sums up what I am saying, it is this.

Rule 104: *Success teaches you about yourself. Failure teaches you about everything else! -* **Anne Beon**

Rule 105: It's better to be a living activist than a dead candidate.

Sadly, my run for office came to an abrupt halt. During the summer of 2015, I was diagnosed with Congestive Heart Failure - early stage. I take my meds on a regular basis. However, while nothing has gotten worse, nothing is much better except for the blood pressure. It was 175/96 and is now at 120/79, though it can fluctuate. I talked this over with

my son and spouse. We all agreed. The
campaign had to end.

I am actually okay with this. Governor
Cuomo has used his Executive Powers to bring
forth much of what was on my platform. Yes, it
still needs to be codified. However, for the
moment, I finally have legal protections here in
New York State.

When I am protected across the land, then I
will say that I am Free!

Rule 106: *If somebody offers you an amazing*
   opportunity but you are not sure you can do
   it, say yes - then learn how to do it later. -
   Sir Richard Branson

As I write this, there are a couple amazing
opportunities that could be presenting
themselves in the very near future. It depends
on Grant Monies. I have absolutely no idea
how to do either of them, but that is not going

to stop me from trying. If offered either opportunity, I will grab it with both hands and go along for the ride!

I mean, let's be honest for a second. I am about to be 59 and I have heart & health issues. I started off at the maximum level for all my medications, so there isn't anything that can be ramped up. If I don't do it now, it isn't gonna happen.

Rule 107: *It takes courage to become who you really are. - e.e.* **cumings.**

This quote isn't so much for me as it is for my partner. I started off dating a woman. Raky then came out as Gender Fluid. Now, it appears that I will have a husband instead of a wife.

No, it is not perfectly smooth sailing. Rocky makes sudden, quantum leaps in his transition. It takes me more than a little bit to play catch-up so I can be on the same page. More importantly, I *want* to be on the same page. Sometimes, it just takes a little bit to get there.

It has been a wonder watching Rocky blossom into the man he has always been inside! His self confidence has been growing by leaps and bounds - that is how I know that he is on the right path.

There are those who say that this is Karma getting back at me. I disagree.

Back then, my first marriage was already crumbling. A strong breeze would have cause it to fail. My coming out simply ensured the destruction of something that was already ending.

The question I have to ask myself is this. Am I a lesbian, or am I hetero? The impact of that question is tremendous.

Rule 108: *Being deeply loved by someone gives you strength, while loving someone deeply gives you courage.* **- Lao Tzu**

I cannot agree more with this. Ever since Rocky and I became a couple, I have found my strength and courage just increasing by incalculable amounts.

Rule 109: *Girls should never be afraid to be smart.* **- Emma Watson**

Rule 110: *Brainy is the new sexy.* **- Irene Adler, *Sherlock***

No woman of any age should be afraid to be smart. No woman should feel like she has to act weak and helpless to find love. Having lived on both sides of the gender aisle, I will tell you this. Most men are attracted to a woman who is strong and intelligent.

Rule 111: *Don't forget to breathe. -* **The Silent Monk,** *The Forbidden Kingdom*

Rule 112: *If one does not attach himself to people and desires, never shall his heart be broken - but then, does he ever truly live? I would rather die a mortal, who has a care for someone, than to live as a man free from his own death. -* **Lu Yan,** *The Forbidden Kingdom*

The truth in this is just profound for me. I know someone whose heart has been shattered and has sworn off relationships. For me, that is existing, not really living. I would rather accept the risk of pain that comes with love than to live in emotional isolation.

Rule 113: *It is like water. Nothing is softer than water, yet it can overcome rock. It does not fight. It flows around the opponent.* **- The Silent Monk,** *The Forbidden Kingdom*

Rule 114: *Formless. Nameless. The true master dwells within. Only you can free him.* **- Lu Yan,** *The Forbidden Kingdom*

Rule 115: *Now, bring me that horizon!* **- Captain Jack Sparrow,** *Pirates of the Caribbean - Curse of the* **Black Pearl.**

As I am editing this, much has happened. Rocky and I separated late 2016. I love him to death, but the simple fact is that I am a lesbian. His transition became a bridge too far for me. (*A Bridge Too Far*. What a great title for a book and movie! Too bad Cornelius Ryan already wrote it.) I had a relationship afterward that may have been a rebound. It was brief, intense, and it seriously messed with my head.

To help center myself, I moved from Rochester to the Finger Lakes Area of New York State. I find the lakes very calming, and I have found myself again.

As I write in 2018, the horizon is still calling my name. It urges me to venture out beyond the safety of the harbor. Go back and look at Rule 39.

I am planning a trip back to Canada for Pride in 2019. For me, it's going Home. Right now, I don't know if I will come back to the United States to stay or not. Much will depend on the 2018 elections.

But how can I abandon my People?

Some historian in the future will look back on this time period and say that this is when the U.S. recovered to be a beacon of light and hope, or that this is when the States stopped being united as the country falls into decay.

Rule 116: *Make your choice. Are you ready to be strong? -* **Buffy,** *Buffy the Vampire Slayer*

Standing up and making a stand is not easy. Nor is it safe. It means sailing into harm's way. However, our fight for Freedom and Equality calls on us to make that choice.

Rule 117: *In every revolution, there is one man with a vision. -* **Captain James T. Kirk,** *Star Trek - Mirror, Mirror.*

That 'man' is often a Woman!

Rule 118: *There are times when a corps commander's life does not count. -* **Major General Winfield Scott Hancock**

It was the third day of the Battle of Gettysburg. July 4, 1863. The Confederate forces started an artillery barrage on the center of the Union Line. It would lead to the Confederate bloodbath known as Picket's Charge.

As everyone dove for cover, General Hancock calmly rode up and down the line talking with his soldiers. Making sure they had cover.

A soldier ran up to the General and begged him to take cover. Hancock said no. He knew being calm in front of his men was the only way to keep up their morale and courage. He knew that it wasn't his life that would save the day, but the lives of his troops. It worked and the Union won the battle.

Rule 119: *There are only two creatures of any value on the face of the Earth. Those with the commitment, and those who require the* *commitment of others.* - **John Adams**

Rule 120: *Men don't follow titles, they follow courage.* - **William Wallace,** *Braveheart*

Rule 121: *Never doubt that a small group of thoughtful, committed citizens can change the world; indeed, it's the only thing that ever has.* - **Margaret Mead**

Rule 122: *Great men do not seek power. They have power thrust upon them!* - **Kahless the Undeniable**

Rules 116 through 122, as well as Rule 89, talk about how living for an ideal is far more important than ones own life. That dedication to achieving that singular ideal draws others to you. They look to you for leadership. Guidance. Courage.

You might never have wanted the job or the responsibility. It's still yours. It's been thrust upon you.

Do you have that Vision? Are you ready to be Strong? Do you have the Commitment? Do you believe that you can change the world for the better? Are you willing to put *everything* on the line to achieve it?

Are you ready to draw that line in the sand?

Rule 123: *One free man defending his home is more powerful than ten hired soldiers. -* **Robin of Locksley,** *Robin Hood, Prince of Thieves*

We are a Free People! We fight to protect our nation, our state, our homes.

We fight to protect our bodies and our right to choose who we are. Remember this -

We are FREE! Never forget that!

If you truly believe in your heart that we are free, we WILL win our Freedom!

Rule 124: *I've spent a life chasing stories to tell when I am old.* **- Atticus**

I have had adventures to last a dozen lifetimes. Some good. Some not so much.

I would not trade away a single adventure for even one extra minute of life.

Last Rule: Doors are meant to be opened – not hidden behind. Go forth and conquer!

Being out as a transperson is one of the hardest gigs in town. It will test your mettle down to its core.

While my life has been difficult these past few years, it has been a walk in the park compared to the lives of Transpeople of Color and Transgender Latinx.

The Transgender Community crosses every culture, race, economic, and social level. We are everywhere and always have been.

This fight for Equality and Justice is a fight for every minority.

We are not going to be pushed around any more.

There are those who look at us as "snowflakes." That we will melt away crying boo hoo hoo at the first sign of trouble.

Clearly, these haters, both men and women, do not understand just who we are. They don't understand what we have been willing to sacrifice to be Authentic.

Let me make this crystal clear.

THESE COLORS DON'T RUN!

Shauna Marie O'Toole shares her journey with audiences both large and small. Shauna is, among other things, a mom, author and outreach educator. She is also a certified LGBTQ Safe Space trainer.

She has started her own nonprofit organization called the *We Exist Coalition of the Finger Lakes* to do outreach and promote visibility for the Transgender / Gender Expansive Community.

She can be reached at the following email: WeExistCoalitionFLX@gmail.com. You can also follow her on Twitter @Shauna_WeExist.

Among her books are:

<u>Non-Fiction:</u>

You Can't Shave In A Minimart Bathroom
(Updated 2013)

Da Rules – The First One Hundred Plus
Lessons I Learned In My Transition.
(Updated 2018)

<u>Fiction:</u>

Recycled.

Exodus

New Frontiers

www.ingramcontent.com/pod-product-compliance
Lightning Source LLC
Chambersburg PA
CBHW020407290526
45785CB00005B/2464